"OUR LOVE HAS GROWN WITH THE TENDERNESS OF A SUMMER'S BREEZE."

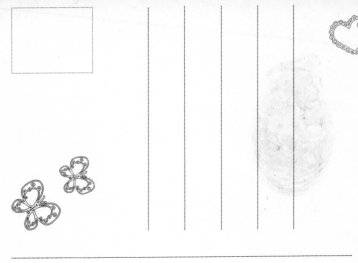

"WHEN I AM WITHOUT YOU I TRACE YOUR FACE IN THE AIR AND WATCH YOU SMILE BACK AT ME."

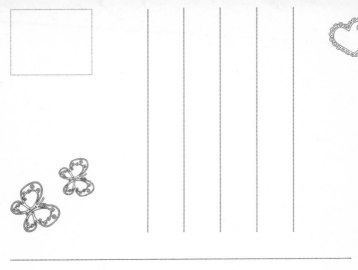

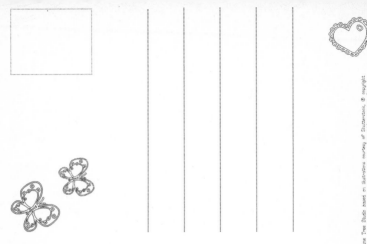

"SUCH SOFT, SWEET SMILES ARE MADE FROM YOUR GENTLE STRENGTHS"

LOVE CAN TAKE MANY FORMS, FROM A RAGING GLORY TO THE QUIET ROAR OF SHY INTROSPECTION.